A Handfull of Herbs

Pub. Nov. 15

Who would therefore looke dangerously up at Planets
That might safely looke downe at Plants?

John Gerard, *The Herball* 1597

D0353471

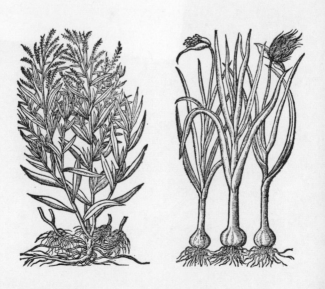

A Handfull of Herbs

Gathered by Gordon Taylor

Blond & Briggs

For The Other Jolly Herb Farmers
Guy Cooper and
John Williamson

Grateful thanks to
Mrs Moyra Burnett, Landscape Designer,
Mrs Barbara Keen, Valeswood Herb Farm,
A. P. Paterson NDH MED FLS
Curator, Chelsea Physic Garden

Illustrations from
The Herball or Generall History of Plants
by John Gerard, 1597

First published in Great Britain 1976
by Blond & Briggs Ltd., London and Tiptree,
Colchester, Essex
Designed by Humphrey Stone and
Printed in Great Britain by
The Compton Press Ltd, The Old Brewery
Tisbury, Salisbury
in Linotype Granjon
on Design Cartridge
© copyright 1976 Tumblers Bottom
Herb Farm Ltd.

ISBN 0 85634 058 8

Introduction

Gordon Taylor's *Handfull of Herbs* hardly
numbers four dozen : they are representative,
however, of a vast number of plants which, since
earliest times, were used by Man to be of service to
him in various ways. This 'handfull' encompasses
the range of herbs from dread Aconite – to which
if taken in quantity there is no known antidote, to
Basil, that most delicious of culinary complements.
Every writer or grower, and Mr. Taylor is both,
will make his own selection : here are his.

But what is a herb ? Botanically it is any plant
which is *herbaceous*; that is, one which dies down
to the ground at the end of its life or at the end of
each season. It cannot possess woodiness; hence
Sage, Lavender, Bay and Lad's Love are not herbs.
Which obviously indicates that botanical categories
have no place in this discussion; those four are
epitomes of herb-ness. So to try again.

Herbs are plants used by Man, but less as food
plants in their own right, which indicates a need
for quantity, than in a qualitative fashion. Many,
of course, are, or were, directly medicinal. Others,
the culinary herbs, have an additive role. In times
when food was ill-kept or positively rotten, ability
to disguise was an invaluable virtue. Today this is
hopefully unnecessary, yet without the comple-
mentariness of herbs much modern food can be
equally offensive.

In the garden herbs fulfil a third function. They
quicken the senses. Nothing is more evocative than
smell, and the merest whiff of Rosemary or
Lily-of-the-Valley can recall times or places past
as effectively as any Proustian 'recherche'.
Visually, too, the range of subtle colour and texture
is unsurpassed; their fourth role is purely and
proudly ornamental.

So as herbs themselves can titillate, so too does this little book. It does not pretend to be definitive but its sources are as varied as the subject. It uses, as have all writers on herbs since 1597, *The Herball* of John Gerard. (He, however, was a patent plagiarist, choosing a title to indicate both originality and definitiveness. Gerard does admit that he 'perused divers herbals set foorth in other languages', but not that of his 1800 illustrative woodcuts, only 16 were original.)

Herbs, it seems, are of perpetual interest, and rightly so, and are continually written about. One should, incidentally, doubt any book dealing with plants — and with herbs in particular — that dares call itself *The Complete Book of* . . . or *All About* . . . : they never can be. Gordon Taylor wisely avoids such false omnisciences; he shows forty-one as the gateway to the rest.

September 1976

ALLEN PATERSON
Curator, Chelsea Physic Garden

Aconite

Aconitum napellus
Greek : Akontion (dart)
The Queen Mother of Poisons
Old Wife's Hood
Helmet Flower
Wolf's Bane
Monk's Hood

Perennial   Height : 600-900 mm

Although a deadly poison, it is most beneficial
medicinally for nerve and chest ailments

Children should be warned against aconite as all
parts of it are poisonous, especially the root

'I have heard that Aconite
being timely taken
hath a healing might,
against the scorpion's stroke'   *Ben Jonson*

It has been listed in English herbals since the
10th century

Other varieties : Aconitum anglicum, chinensis,
japonicum and many more which are spread widely
over the world

Grows best in moist, shady positions

Angelica

Angelica archangelica
Garden Angelica
The Root of the Holy Ghost

Biennial but may be perennial if flowers removed
Height: 1200-1800 mm

'It cureth the bitings of mad dogges
and all other venomous beasts'   *Gerard*

It has been held in highest esteem for centuries
in many countries for both culinary and medicinal
properties: digestive tea, and a good remedy for
colds, coughs, pleurisy and rheumatism

A confectionery flavouring and decoration – the
candied stalks; and used in the preparation of
gin, vermouth and chartreuse; also good in jams
and with rhubarb

Purportedly dispels lust in younger persons

Likes moist, well-drained, fairly rich
soil and partial shade

Apothecary's Rose

Rosa gallica officinalis
The Rose of Lancaster
The Rose of Provins

Perennial   Height: 1200-1800 mm

The oldest rose known to Man having originated
from Persia

Many uses in medicine, cosmetics and food:
Honey or Syrup of Rose for coughs; Ointment
of Rose as a cold cream; in confectionery
and in liqueurs such as *L'Huile de Rose* and
Parfait-Amour

'Of their sweet death
are sweetest odours made'   *William Shakespeare*

Dried petals of scented roses are a major
ingredient in pot-pourri

Rose petal rounds have been recommended as
a slightly *raffiné* alternative to cucumber
sandwiches

It thrives on poor soil and prefers sun;
the double, richly scented flowers come in
June-July

Balm

Melissa officinalis
Greek: Melissa (honey bee)
Bawme
Lemon Balm
Sweet Balm

Perennial   Height: 600-900 mm

The word Balm is an abbreviation for Balsam,
chief of the ancient sweet oils

A fragrant furniture polish in renaissance times

The lemony taste is good in poultry stuffing,
fish and stews, and for summer drinks, wine cups
and salads

'An essence of Balm, given in Canary wine,
every morning will renew youth, strengthen
the brain, relieve languishing nature and
prevent baldness'   *The London Dispensary*, 1691

Bee hives rubbed with it keep the bees at home

Golden Lemon Balm is the variegated type

Grows in almost any garden situation and can be
propagated by seeds, cuttings or roots in
Spring or Autumn; caution: it can invade like
mint and horseradish

Black Peppermint

Mentha piperita vulgaris
France: Menthe de Notre Dame
Italy: Erba Santa Maria

Perennial   Height: 300-600 mm

A symbol of virtue

Referred to by St. Luke as the tithe-mint which
the Jews were commanded to pay

'Astringent and of warm subtle parts – great
strengthener of the stomach'   *Culpeper*

It has one of the essential oils used in toothpastes,
digestives, confectionery and liqueurs

The Arabs believe that mint improves virility

Some other varieties of mint: Bowles, *Eau-de-
Cologne*, Garden and Ginger

Needs rich, moist soil and partial shade

Catmint

Nepeta cataria
Catnep

Perennial   Height: 300-600 mm

English peasantry brewed a tea from it before
the imports from China

'If you set it, cats will eat it,
if you sow it, the cats don't know it!'

The tea is a valuable treatment for every type
of fever; recommended for hysteria, headaches
and nightmares

'The juice drunk in wine is good for bruises
and the green leaves bruised and made into an
ointment is effectual for piles'   *Culpeper*

A rat repellent

Chewing its root will supposedly give one a
dose of courage

The Pennsylvania Dutch offered the tea as an
appetite stimulant

Dry, sandy soil in full sun gives most fragrance

Chervil

Anthriscus cerefolium
Poor Man's Tarragon

Annual: but self seeding   Height: 300-900 mm

A native of Russia and Western Asia

A Roman prescription against hiccoughs was
chervil seeds and vinegar

One of the oldest seasoning plants in Europe
and brought to Britain by the Romans

An ingredient of *Fines Herbes* and it is a sweet
and spicy alternative to parsley. Béarnaise
sauce requires it and it is also a main
ingredient in the classic potato soup

Can be sown all year round, does not like to be
transplanted and prefers light soil, to be
watered regularly, and somewhat shaded as
direct sun will bleach the leaves; suitable
for indoors or window boxes

Chives

Allium schoenoprasum
Old English: Cives
Old French: Petit poureau
French: Ail Civitte
Rush-Leek
Infant Onion

Perennial   Height: 150-250 mm

China was probably the country of origin a
few thousand years ago, and first cultivated
in Europe during the Middle Ages

Now native to the cooler parts of Western
Europe, including England

The smallest member of the onion family which
also includes Garlic, Leek, Shallot, Welsh
and Tree Onions

Delicate onion flavour enhances omelettes,
salads, tomato dishes and young vegetables,
such as petit pois

Pennsylvania Dutch settlers in America pastured
their cows in chive fields and invented
Philadelphia Cream Cheese?

Another variety is Giant Chives

Can be cultivated in ordinary, well-drained
garden soil and harvested continually

Comfrey

Symphytum officinale
Knitbone
Bruisewort
Consolida
Ass Ear
Abraham, Isaac and Joseph
Church Bells
Coffee Flower
Gooseberry Pie
Pigweed
Snake and Suckers

Perennial   Height: 600-900 mm

An ancient wound herb

'A Salve concocted from the fresh herb will certainly tend to promote healing of bruised and broken parts'   *Gerard*

A valuable addition to compost for those of the organic persuasion

Makes a strong tea for internal haemorrhage

English country people have cultivated it in their gardens for centuries

Young leaves once used in salads and made into fritters

Some other varieties: Russian, English, Caucasian and Dwarf Variegated

Thrives in almost any soil, and when established it can be very difficult to eradicate

Cowslip

Primula veris
Greek : Paralysio
Anglo-Saxon : Cuy lippe
Crewel
Paigle
Fairy Cups
Herb Peter
Our Lady's Keys

Perennial   Height : 150 mm

Cowslip wine or cordial is not only delicious but
has sedative properties. Traditionally used for
strengthening nerves and relieving insomnia

'In their gold coats spots you see,
These be rubies fairy favours
In those freckles lie their savours'
Midsummer Night's Dream

'Tosties' or Cowslip Balls were made
from the flowers by country children

'Some women we find, sprinkle ye floures of
cowslip w^t whyte wine and after still it and
wash their faces w^t that water to drive
wrinkles away and to make them fayre in the
eyes of the worlde rather than in the eyes of
God, whom they are not afrayd to offend!'
William Turner

Close relatives are Primrose and Oxlip

Grows wild in woods and moist pastures and
shows in April–May

Fennel

Foeniculum officinale
Old English: Fenkel
Somerset: Spignel
Green Fennel
Sweet Fennel

Perennial   Height: 1500 mm

Traditionally taken to improve eyesight and
the waistline

'To sow Fennel is to sow sorrow'

Superb for all fish dishes and in salads,
cheese spreads and soups

Focniculum vulgare dulce, Finnochio or
Florence Fennel produces the large bulbs
used as a vegetable or in salads

'In Fennel seed this vertue you shall find,
Foorth your lower parts to drive the winde'
                    The Englishman's Doctor, 1608

Bronze Fennel is the decorative relative

Easy to grow and thrives in almost any soil;
a handsome background plant

Foxglove

Digitalis purpurea
Old French: Gantes nostre dame
Folk's Glove
Gloves of Our Lady
Dead Men's Bells
Fairy Thimbles
Bloody Fingers
Fairy Caps

Biennial   Height: 900-1200 mm

The leaves and seeds are used as a major cardiac
stimulant. And, if the digitalis fails, then
herbalists recommend Lily-of-the-Valley

Culpeper declared: 'I am confident that an
ointment of it is one of the best remedies for a
scabby head that is'; considered one of the many
cures for the famed '*King's Evil*'

Highly poisonous itself, but purportedly an
antidote for aconite poisoning

'Foxglove boiled in water or wine, and drunken,
doth cut and consume the thicke toughnesse of
grosse and slimie flegme and naughtie humours'
                                                    Gerard

Does best in well-drained loose soil on hot,
sunny banks protected by a woodland

French Parsley

Carum petroselinum hortense
Petersylinge
Persele
Persley

Biennial   Height : 225-300 mm

In ancient times, it was sacred to
victorious athletes and the tombs
of the dead

Substitute for and superior to the curled
type – both used in *Fines Herbes* and *Bouquets Garnis*

As with sage, it prospers only where the wife
rules

'If you will have the leaves of the parcelye grow
crisped, then before the sowing of them stuffe a
tennis ball with the sedes and beat the same well
against the ground whereby the sedes may be a
little bruised . . .'   *Gerard*

Parsley tea is used for rheumatism and kidney
ailments

Curled and Hamburg are the two other major
types

A moist, partially shaded growing situation
is best

French Tarragon

Artemisia dracunculus
Arabic: Tarkhun (dragon)
Greek: Drakon
French: Herbe au dragon
Little Dragon

Perennial   Height: 300-600 mm

Related to the wormwood used in making absinthe

True french tarragon is one of the great
culinary herbs, essential to the classic
French dishes: Tarragon Chicken and
Béarnaise Sauce; with eggs, in sauces and
for *Fines Herbes*

Introduced into Britain about 1548 when William
Turner first mentioned it in one of his herbals

The root was once used as a toothache remedy

''Tis highly cordial and friend to the head,
heart and liver' *Evelyn*

Often confused with its bland relative
Russian Tarragon, Artemisia dracunculoides

Prefers poor soil, sunny position, needs some
winter protection in Northern climates

Garden Sorrel

Rumex acetosa
Bread and Cheese
Brown Sugar
Soldiers
Gypsy's Baccy
Sour Dock
Sour Sodge
Cuckoo's Meat
Tom Thumb's Thousand Fingers

Perennial   Height: 600-900 mm

The traditional rural Green Sauce for cold meats
was mashed sorrel mixed with vinegar and sugar

'The leaves of Sorrel coole the sick body and
quench thirst'   *Gerard*

The acid flavour is a good contrast to fish,
roast pork, veal or lamb and a delicious
salad leaf; can be cooked as a vegetable

'In the making of sallets imparts a grateful
quickness to the rest as supplying, the want
of oranges and lemons'   *Evelyn*

French Sorrel has the more delicate flavour,
and is major to the famous *Soupe aux Herbes*

Grows best in damp situation

Garlic

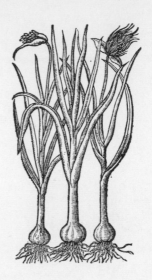

Allium sativum
Poor Man's Treacle

Perennial   Height: 600 mm

Of such antiquity, it is difficult to trace
its country of origin

Records from ancient Egypt show that it was
eaten by the slaves who built the pyramids

Believed to have cured leprosy and smallpox;
and is good for earache

'When Satan stepped out from the garden of
Eden after the Fall, Garlick sprang up from the
spot where he placed his left foot, the Onion
from that where his right touch'd'

Anonymous

Scientists at a Californian University have
recently found garlic extract to be a most
effective mosquito killer

The culinary uses are obvious and legion:
from the *Aioli* of Provence, to scenting a salad
bowl

Grows best in full sun and enriched
sandy ground

Hellebore

Helleborus niger
Black Hellebore
Christe Herbe
Christmas Rose

Perennial Evergreen   Height: 600-900 mm

'Strewed upon fouled ulcers it eats away the
dead flesh, and instantly heals them. Best
being purified by the alchemist than given raw'
Culpeper

A poisonous plant found wild in many parts of
England with powerful medicinal properties –
nervous disorders and hysteria

'A purgation of Hellebore is good for mad and
furious men, and those molested with
melancholy' *Gerard*

'Borage and Hellebore fill two scenes, sovreign
plants to purge the veins of melancholy, and
cheer the heart of those black fumes which
make it smart!'
Robert Burton, Anatomy of Melancholy

Some other varieties: Helleborus foetidus,
viridis, corsicus and orientalis: the Lenten Rose

Needs moist sheltered position with partial shade

Horehound

Marrubium vulgare
Hebrew: Marrob, a bitter juice
French: Marrube
Italian: Marrubio

Perennial   Height: 300-600 mm

'Horehound is bitter to the palate, and yet
sweet to drink. Drink Horehound hot from the
fire if you are poisoned by your step-mother'
English Monk, 9th century

Gypsies use the plant as a fly repellent

Basis of Horehound Candy, and a brew called
Horehound Ale was once popular in Norfolk

'Syrup made of the Green fresh leaves and sugar
is a most singular remedie against the cough
and wheezing of the lungs'   *Gerard*

Main ingredients of a herbal tobacco are
horehound and coltsfoot

The other variety is Black Horehound

A hardy plant which does best in poor, dry soil

Lad's Love

Artemisia abrotanum
French: Garde Robe or Armoise
Scottish: Appleringie
Welsh: Rabbit Tobacco
Southernwood
Old Man
Maidens' Ruin
Stabwort
Boy's Love

Perennial   Height: 600-900 mm

Sprays carried in church to prevent drowsiness

Called 'Garde Robe' for it can be used as a
moth repellent

Used as an ointment by country lads to promote
beard growth

'The ashes mingled with old salad oil helps the
hair to grow again, either on the head or beard'
Culpeper

Also used in love potions and love philtres

Old Lady, Old Warrior, Ladies' Maid, French and
Russian Tarragon, Wormwood and Mugwort
are all members of the Artemisia tribe

Prefers a sandy, well-drained soil in a sunny
position

Lady's Mantle

Alchemilla vulgaris
Arabic: Alkemelych
French: Pied-de-Lion
German: Frauenmantle
Bear's Foot
Nine Hooks
Lion's Foot

Perennial   Height: 300 mm

This herb claimed by Venus and known as a
'Woman's best friend'

Of a very drying and binding character and
one of the best wound herbs

'Helps women who have over flagging breasts,
causing them to grow less and hard, both when
drunk and outwardly applied   *Culpeper*

A major flower and plant of alchemy

Extremely hardy, self-sowing and will survive
in almost any moist, well-drained soil in either
sun or partial shade

Lily-of-the-Valley

Convallaria majalis
French: Muguet de Bois
May Lily
Our Lady's Tears
Lily Constancy
Ladder-to-Heaven
Male Lily

Perennial Height: 150-225 mm

The leaves yield a green dye

The dainty flower is presented in France as a
love token on the first day of May

Always grows where a saint has died

'The floures of May Lillies put into a glasse and set
in a hill of Antes close stopped for the space of a
moneth and then taken out, therein you shall find
a liquor that appeaseth the paine and griefe of the
gout, being outwardly applied, which is
commended to be most excellent'

Gerard

Lily-of-the-Valley is quite easy to cultivate
in well-drained sandy loam and likes shade

Lovage

Levisticum officinale
German: Leibstockel
Love Parsley
Old English Lovage
Italian Lovage
Cornish Lovage

Perennial   Height: 900-1500 mm

Romans brought it to Great Britain and until
the 19th century it was much grown in English
gardens

Has a yeasty celery flavour – good in stews,
soups, salads and mayonnaise

Mixed with Yarrow and Tansy and Brandy
it makes the famous West Country tipple: Lovage
Cordial

A very potent herb and was once used as a
deodorant and a bath refreshment

Grows wild by the sea in areas of Northumberland
and Scotland

Easy to cultivate; it likes a rich, moist
soil and an open, sunny position

Lungwort

Pulmonaria officinalis
Adam and Eve
Spotted Virgin
Jerusalem Cowslip
Spotted Comfrey
Soldiers and Sailors

Perennial   Height: 400-450 mm

'An excellent remedy boiled in beer for
broken-winded horses'   *Culpeper*

Flowers are pink initially, then turn a violet blue
as they open

Its reputation for curing lung and chest
disorders arose not from its medicinal
effectiveness, but from the lung-like appearance
of the leaves; based on a medieval notion of
The Doctrine of Signatures: identifying an
organ of the body with the shape or colours of a
plant: Navelwort, Hepatica and yellow flowers
to treat Jaundice, etc., etc.

Oak Lungs or Lung Moss, Sticta pulmonaria,
is the plant used for properly treating chest
complaints

Needs moisture and shade in ordinary soil

Meadowsweet

Filipendula ulmaria
Queen of the Meadow
Dolloff
Bridewort
Courtship-and-Matrimony
Kiss-me-Quick
May of the Meadow
New Mown Hay
Queen's Feather
Summer's Farewell

Perennial   Height: 600-1200 mm

The three herbs held most sacred by the Druids
were Meadowsweet, Water-Mint and Vervain

It was a major medieval and renaissance strewing
herb; 'The leaves and floures of Meadowsweet
farre excelle all other strewing herbs for to
decke up houses, to strawe in chambers, halls
and banqueting-houses in the Summer-time, for
the smell thereof makes the heart merrie and
joyful and delighteth the senses'   *Gerard*

A strange quality of this herb is that the leaves
and flowers have a very different scent, hence
the name Courtship-and-Matrimony

The mead or honey-wine herb; the flowers were
put into wine and beer. It is still incorporated
in herb beers

Rejoices in growing on moist banks and in
meadows with partial shade

Old English Lavender

Lavandula spica
Latin: Lavandus (to be washed)

Perennial Height: 900-1200 mm

Native of France and Spain and was much
cultivated in English monasteries

'To perfume linnen, apparell, gloves and leather
and the dryed flowers to comfort and dry up
the moisture of a cold braine' *Parkinson*

Dried herb essential in pot-pourri and sachets

Oil has strong antiseptic properties; a tea made
from flowers is a remedy for hysteria, fainting,
giddiness and headache

'Here's your sweet Lavender,
Sixteen sprigs a penny,
Which you will find, my ladies,
Will smell as sweet as any' *London Street Cry*

Other varieties include: Hidcote, Seal, White,
Pink, Dutch and Grappenhall

Bees love all forms of lavender and they are
good sources of nectar

Best planting position is well-drained and sunny

Pennyroyal Mint

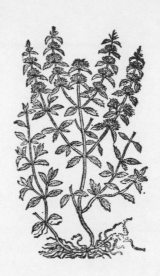

Mentha pulegium
Run-by-the-Ground
Pudding Grass
Lungmint
Fleamint
Lurk-in-the-Ditch

Perennial   Height: 150-225 mm

A Roman flea repellent and a mosquito
repellent for the Arabs

Medicinally used for abortions

Witches employ it for casting spells and
Pennyroyal is a flavouring in Black or
Blood Pudding

'Pennyroyal and mints together, help those who
swoon and faint, if smelled at or put into
the mouth' *Culpeper*

Pilgrim settlers introduced it to North America

'The Pennyroyal of grace divine
   In little cradles they do weave,
Little cradles therewith they line
   On Christmas Eve'

Its natural habitat is moist heaths and
beside ponds

Periwinkle

Vinca minor
Old English: Perwynke
Italian: Fiore di Morte
French: Violette des Sorciers
Ground Ivy
Pennywinkle
Joy of the Ground

Evergreen Perennial   Height 75-275 mm and
recumbent length 900-1200 mm

To the Germans it is the Flower of Immortality

Herbalists today use it for the treatment of
haemorrhages and diabetes; tests show it to be
a rich source of many alkaloids

'The young tops made into a conserve is good
for the nightmare'   *Gerard*

Heretics were crowned with periwinkle before
being burnt at the stake

'Through primrose tufts in that sweet bower
The fair periwinkle trailed its wreaths'
William Wordsworth

Likes well-drained fertile soil and shady
position

Rosemary

Rosmarinus officinalis
Old French: Incensier
Spanish: Romero
Rosmarinus coronarium
Dew of the Sea
Polar Plant
Compass Weed

Evergreen Perennial   Height: 1200-1500 mm

'As for Rosemarine, I lett it runne all over my garden walls, not onlie because my bees love it, but because it is the herb sacred to remembrance and, therefore, to friendship'

Sir Thomas More

The main ingredient for Queen of Hungary Water of the 13th century; also called Spirit of Rosemary

'Grow it for two ends,
it matters not at all,
Be't for my bridall
or my buriall' *Robert Herrick*

Used sparingly it can be delicious with lamb and other roasted meats

Other varieties include: Corsican Blue, Golden or Gilded, Miss Jessop, Prostrate and Seven Seas

Grows best in light soil and sunny position; wet or heavy soils are not good

Royal Fern

Osmunda regalis
Osmund-royal
Osmund the Waterman
Water Fern
Heart of Osmund

Perennial   Height: 1200-1500 mm

Named after a Saxon Prince, Osmund, whose name meant domestic peace

Royal Fern Jelly was extracted from the root and sweetened with honey, wine and spices. It was a special medicine given to young princes of the royal house of France

'Good for those that have fallen from some high place' *Gerard*

The roots are used today commercially as orchid compost

Plant found world-wide, except Australasia, and it is the tallest of British ferns

It has been dedicated to St. Christopher

Enjoys partial shade in rich, humus soil, easy to cultivate

Rue

Ruta graveolens
Greek : Reuo (to set free)
Herb of Grace
Herbygrass
Garden Rue

Perennial   Height: 600-900 mm

Cherished by the Arabs because it is the only
herb said to have been blessed by Mohamet

> 'Here in this place
> I'll set a bank of rue, sour herb of grace;
> Rue, even for ruth, here shortly shall be seen,
> In the remembrance of a weeping Queen'
> *Richard II*

Antidote for poisons, epilepsy, vertigo and
helpful for sharp and clear eyesight; drunk as a
tea in Wales

'The Weasel when she is to encounter the serpent
arms herself with eating of Rue' *Coles*

In Italy a sprig flavours salads and the fire
water, *Grappa*

Some varieties are Variegated and Jackmans Blue

Grows anywhere, but best in dry sheltered
positions

Sage

Salvia officinalis
Latin: Salvere (to be saved)
Old English: Sawge
Green Sage
Sage the Saviour

Evergreen Perennial   Height: 600-750 mm

The Romans called it 'herba sacra' and also mixed
it with cheese

'Gargles are made with Sage, Rosemary,
Honeysuckles and Plantains boiled in wine
or water with some honey or alum. *Culpeper*

Green Sage is used in poultry stuffings and with
goose and pork because of its digestive qualities

'He that would live for aye,
must eat Sage in May'

Sage tea was once highly valued by the Chinese

In Sussex in the old days, sage eaten on nine
mornings while fasting was the rural cure for
ague

Red or Purple, Golden and Tri-Colour are
decorative types

Flourishes in rich clay loam – good drainage and
full sun

Soapwort

Saponaria officinalis
Bouncing Bet
Latherwort
Crow Soap
Sweet Betty
Fuller's Herb

Perennial   Height: 900-1500 mm

A decoction cures the itch

Used in the 16th century for treatment of
French-Poxes

'It is commonly called Saponaria, of the great
scourging qualitie of the leaves have; for they
yield out of themselves a certain juice when
they are bruised as well good as sope'   *Gerard*

A valuable remedy for rheumatism or skin troubles
due to any form of venereal disease

Medicinally it has a detergent action and is
good for all skin diseases

In the 20th century it was re-discovered as the
finest soap for cleaning delicate tapestries,
old fabrics and restoring original colours

Grows wild by brooks and the sea in a sunny
position

Stinking Gladwyn

Iris foetidissima
Spurgewort
Spurge Plant
Roast Beef Plant
Gladwin
Stinking Gladdon

Perennial   Height: 300-600 mm

A wild plant found in many parts of England particularly the south-west and used as a purgative

One of the many herbs useful against the '*King's Evil*', or Scrofula, which formerly was supposed to be cured by the touch of a '*Royal*'

Dried root also used for hysterical disorders and fainting

Dedicated to the Goddess Juno

'It helpeth Buboes in the groine, as Pliny saith' *Gerard*

The plant has a long and honourable history in medicine being referred to by Theophrastus, 4th century B.C.

Found in hedgerows and on shady banks

Sweet Basil

Ocymum basilicum
Greek: Basileus (king)

Annual in England   Height: 225-300 mm

Originally came from India where it was used
to cleanse temples; imported to Europe in
the 16th century

'The physical properties are to procure a
cheerful and merry hearte whereunto the seed
is chiefly used in powder . . . but being hardly
wrung and bruised would breed scorpions'

Parkinson

Oil of Basil is used in perfumes and the dried
leaves in snuff

Another of the great culinary herbs: all tomato
dishes, eggs, fish and for the *Pesto* sauce of
Italy and the *Pistou* soup of France

Basil and Rue – one of the sweetest and one of
the most bitter of herbs should never be planted
near each other: the theory of companion planting

Other varieties: Bush, Dark Opal or Purple;
and Lettuce-leaf or Crispum

Likes well-drained, rich soil and water at
noon-time

Sweet Bay

Laurus nobilis
French: Laurier d'Apollon
Noble Laurel
Roman Laurel
Lorbeer

Evergreen Perennial   Mature Height: 7500 mm

Greek and Roman symbol of wisdom: crowns for
heroes and poets – Poet Laureate; also dedicated
to the Greek god of medicine, Aesculapius

The sweet-scented wood is used for rather
special marquetry

The antiseptic Oil of Bay is a remedy for
sprains and a tea is made to sharpen the
appetite

Many uses in cooking being a main ingredient
of *Bouquets Garnis*, along with marjoram, parsley
and thyme; also essential for marinades and
court bouillon

American colonists used bay leaves as a
caterpillar repellent

Golden Bay is the handsome variation

Grows best in moderately rich soil; needs
protection from cold winds

Sweet Cicely

Myrrhis odorata
Sweets
Sweet-Cus
British Myrrh
Sweet Chervil
Shepherd's Needle
Wild Chervil

Perennial   Height: 600-900 mm

A valuable tonic for girls from 15 to 18 years of age

The sweet anise flavour is excellent in stewed fruit, trifles and salads

It also reduces acidity in many fruits and the need for sugar or honey; especially good for diabetics and slimmers

Provided a furniture polish with a good gloss and pleasant scent used in the north of England during the 16th and 17th centuries

The old herbalists reckoned it was good for the elderly who were dull and without courage

Difficult to propagate from seed as it needs a long period of winterisation, but grows in ordinary soil and freely re-seeds itself once established

Sweet Marjoram

Origanum majorana
Greek: Rigani (joy of the mountains)
Knotted Marjoram

Annual in England   Height: 300 mm

'Between Marjoram and adders there is a
deadly antipathy'   *Culpeper*

A Greek and Roman custom was to crown young
couples with it

Culinary – in pasta, omelettes, stuffings,
sausages and it is a major alternative to
thyme with meats

In order to find a future partner, having
dried and powdered marigold flowers, thyme,
wormwood and a sprig of marjoram and taken
the concoction and chanted the following three
times:

'St. Luke, St. Luke be kind to me,
in my dreams let my true love see'

then he or she must appear

French or Pot is the perennial form, Compact,
Golden and Wild are some of the other varieties

Can be sown under cover in March and planted
out in May after frosts have gone: not particular
about the type of soil

Tansy

Tanacetum vulgare
Tansye
Buttons

Perennial   Height: 900-1500 mm

Said to be effectual in keeping flies away,
if mixed with elder leaves

In Sussex, tansy leaves purportedly also
cured ague if placed in shoes

Tansies: traditional English post-Lenten cakes
eaten to purify the body after the rigours
of Lent

The scent is not unlike camphor

The plant was dedicated to the Virgin Mary

'Of Tansie, the root eaten, is a singular
remedy for the gout: the rich may bestow
the cost to preserve it' *Culpeper*

An important embalming herb in early days

Tansy will grow in almost any soil and can
be easily propagated by root division

Thyme

Thymus vulgaris
Greek: Thymum (to burn sacrifice)
Common Thyme

Perennial   Height: 100-200 mm

In the 17th century thyme and beer soup was
thought to be a cure for shyness

Thyme, along with parsley and bay, makes up
Bouquets Garnis

Honey bees love it and it is a long revered
symbol of bravery

'Burnet, Wild Thyme and Water-Mints which
perfume the air most delightfully being trodden
upon and crushed' *Sir Francis Bacon*

The essential oil thymol is an ingredient of toothpastes and other pharmaceutical preparations

'Thyme for the Time it lasteth, yieldeth most and
best honie and therefore, in old Time,
was accounted chief' *Anonymous*

Some other varieties are: Azoricus, Doone Valley,
Fragrantissimus, Lemon Curd, Herba-barona,
Pink Chintz, Silver Lemon Queen and Silver
Posie

Poor well-drained stony soil in full sun is best

Winter Savory

Satureia montana

Perennial Evergreen   Height: 300 mm

Its peppery flavour is delicious with fish and
all bean dishes

Said to be effective for colic

Parkinson mentioned that his contemporaries
used it thus: 'to breade their meate, be it
fish or flesh, to give it a quicker relish'

Both Savories contain a strong volatile oil
which aids digestion of cucumber, salads and
pork dishes

Crushed leaves are good for treatment of bee sting

The Savories – both Summer the annual – Satureia
hortensis – and Winter the perennial, were
brought to Britain by the Romans

Happier in a poor soil rather than a rich one

Yarrow

Achillea millefolium
Herbe Militaris
Soldiers' Woundwort
Milfoil
Nose Bleed
Devil's Plaything
Thousand Weed
Bad Man's Plaything

Perennial   Height: 600-900 mm

The genus name derives from a legend that
Achilles staunched his soldiers' wounds with
the plant

Once dedicated to the Devil and used in casting
spells by witches

Its antiseptic properties are many and it is
one of the All-Heal herbs: stomach, kidneys,
heart and skin

The counting of the 49 dried Yarrow stalks is
the traditional method of divining the ancient
Chinese oracular text, *I Ching*, or Book of
Changes

Likes moderately rich, rather moist soil
in full sun

Sources Consulted

Acetaria: A Discourse of Sallets, John Evelyn, London, 1699

A Garden of Herbs, Eleanor Sinclair Rohde, Hale Cushman and Flint, 1936

A Modern Herbal, Mrs. Maude Grieve, Cape, London, 1931

British Botanical and Horticultural Literature before 1800, Blanche Henrey, Oxford University Press, 1975

Food for Free, Richard Mabey, Collins, London, 1972

Green Enchantment: The Magic Spell of Gardens, Rosetta E. Clarkson, Macmillan, New York, 1940

Herbs for Every Garden, Gertrude B. Foster, Dent, London, 1966

Herbs: Their Culture and Uses, Rosetta E. Clarkson, Macmillan, New York, 1942

Herbs to Grow Indoors, Adelma Grenier Simmons, Hawthorn, New York, 1969

Paradisi in Sole, John Parkinson, London, 1629

Potter's Encyclopedia of Botanical Drugs and Preparations, Pitman, London, 1907

Readers Digest Encyclopedia of Garden Plants & Flowers, 1971

The Art of Simpling, William Coles, London, 1656

The Complete Book of Herbs and Spices, Claire Loewenfeld and Phillipa Back, David and Charles, London, 1974

The English Physitian, Nicholas Culpeper, London, 1653

The Herball, John Gerard, 1597

The I Ching, or Book of Changes, Wilhelm/Baynes Translation, Bollingen Series, Pantheon Books, New York, 1950